WRITING PAPERS

A Handbook for Students at Smith College

2nd Revised Edition

by
Joan H. Garrett-Goodyear
Elizabeth W. Harries
Douglas L. Patey
Margaret L. Shook

"The correction of prose, because it has no fixed laws, is endless."
— W. B. Yeats

Sundance Publishing
234 Taylor Street, Littleton, MA 01460

Writing Papers

To the Student:

Good writing is difficult but not mysterious. While we can't turn all students into great writers or great stylists, we hope that this handbook will help you write clear, correct, and forceful prose. Writing well takes practice and hard work. But, unlike genius, it is all perspiration; it does not depend on intuition or inspiration. Good papers are made, not born.

Some handbooks merely list common mistakes and show how to correct them. Correct prose, however, is not always good prose; even a car in perfect mechanical order won't go unless you give it some gas. We will mention some of the mechanical problems that tend to make student writing knock and stall and occasionally even break down, but we will concentrate on helping you give your prose the energy it needs: clarity, point, vitality.

If you learn to give your academic papers this energy, you will find that your other writing — everything from business letters to love letters, from law briefs to lab reports — will also improve. We can't promise that writing will become easier, but we can promise that it will be more satisfying. Writing well forces you to explore your subject thoroughly; it also forces you to explore yourself.

Thanks to Paul Pickrel and Elizabeth von Klemperer, for finding infelicities and stupidities in our early drafts; to Marian Simpson, for comments about tenses and quotations; to Philip Green, for the Northampton/Holyoke example; to Robert Averitt, for suggestions about the logic of economics; to George Fleck, for heroic efforts to make this handbook useful for scientists; to Kenneth McCartney and Jill Conway, for advice, support, and encouragement; to Claudia Kahn, Nellie O'Neil, and their colleagues in the President's Office, for turning our jumbled messes into clear typescript; to Lucinda Brown, for transforming the typed manuscript into an elegant printed pamphlet. And particular thanks to our students for bad examples and good questions.

Joan H. Garrett-Goodyear
Elizabeth W. Harries
Douglas L. Patey
Margaret L. Shook

ISBN 0-88741-098-7

Table of Contents

A grant from Conoco, Incorporated, of Stamford, Connecticut, provided the financial support for the preparation of *Writing Papers*.

I. Putting a Paper Together

A. Getting started

1. Questions. Good papers usually begin with good questions. As you are doing the reading and research for a paper, scribble down your own version of these questions: What has particularly interested me about this subject? What passages in the text have I underlined in my first reading, and is there anything that connects them? (Where you see a pattern of related ideas widely separated in the text, there's often a paper topic.) What has my teacher, or somebody else in the class, or the textbook, or a secondary source said about this topic that I disagree with, or at least find questionable? (Where there's disagreement, there's often a paper topic.) Try to make your questions more and more specific and focused. Stop taking notes every once in a while and ask: How have my questions changed? What will probably be my main question? How will the reading I'm doing now help me answer that question?

2. Drafts. The belief that you write good papers in one intense, creative session can also make it hard to get started. You should think of your first writing as exploratory, as a first rather than as a final version. You will find it easier to begin to write things down if you remind yourself that this is a **draft,** that your first attempts can be changed, reorganized, or even thrown away. No good writer produces perfect copy the first time, and many change their works even after they have been published. (Even great writers blot, cross out, add, and change; take a look at some of their manuscripts.) Someone said once that an eraser, a pair of scissors, and a pot of paste (or a roll of Scotch tape and some correction fluid) are the writer's most important tools. Don't try to do without them.

3. *Free Writing.* Some writers have suggested other ways to get started. Peter Elbow in his *Writing Without Teachers* (New York: Oxford, 1973) has some interesting ideas about free writing as a way to find out what you really have to say. In his free writing exercises, you write for ten minutes about your subject without stopping, without lifting your pen from the paper, without stopping to agonize over word choice or spelling or coherence, just letting ideas flow out. Then you stop and sift the good from the bad, the useful from the useless. Then you repeat the free writing, basing it on what you have salvaged from the first attempt. You repeat the process until you have something you can use to begin your paper. For some people this process may take as many as five increasingly coherent versions; for some people it may never work at all. But it's worth trying when you're having difficulty getting started.

4. *Outlines.* If you have some conception of your general idea and of the evidence you can give for it, an outline is a classic device for getting started. It can give you a framework for your first gropings and can help you organize the material your paper will be based on.

We wrote this handbook, for example, from a rather simple **topic or phrase outline,** an early version of the table of contents on page iii. A more elaborate outline would have more sub-headings:

III. Writing correctly
    A. Sentence structure (syntax)
       1. Dangling modifiers
         a. Separated modifiers
         b. Dangling modifiers at the beginning of sentences
         c. Dangling *which*-clauses
       2. Parallelism

and so on. Notice that in this more detailed outline you show the relative significance of items by their number or letter and by indentation — the more important or general closest to the left-hand margin, the less important or more specific farthest from it.

Sometimes a **sentence outline** is more helpful. When we described this project to our colleagues, we wouldn't just list the topics we were covering, but would say something like: "In the first major section we show how to deal with some problems of focus and organization. In the second section we try to combat some common misconceptions about word choice. In the third . . ." and so on. For a short paper you might want to write a sentence about what each paragraph will do; for a longer paper, you would probably write one sentence for each section.

In an **assertion outline,** you write a sentence summarizing the point of each paragraph or section. This forces you to think carefully about the course your argument is going to take, and to develop each paragraph or section logically in relation to the others. We could have described what we were doing by saying: "The first sub-section, 'Getting started,' shows that, though beginning a paper at all is often difficult, certain techniques can make it easier. The second sub-section, 'Refining your topic; defining your thesis,' shows how to focus a topic once you have found one and to distinguish a topic from a thesis . . ." and so on. (Sometimes a **question outline,** a tentative design for your paper based on the questions you are trying to answer, will be more useful.)

An outline, like a first draft, can always be changed and usually should be. Though we knew approximately what subjects we wanted to cover, for example, their order changed somewhat as we worked. But an outline is always a useful point of reference, even as it changes.

B.   Refining your topic; defining your thesis

Many papers try to cover too much. Trying to discuss the causes of the Civil War in ten pages is trying the impossible; you can achieve a superficial listing at best, never a coherent and fully developed explanation. Limit and refine your topic until you hit on something that you can really explore in detail in the space you have. Learn to distinguish between two-page and ten-page ideas. Force yourself to concentrate on something manageable by choosing a title that limits the focus of your paper:

not "The Causes of the Civil War" **or even** "The Abolitionist Movement" **but** "Two Abolitionist Tracts that Led to the Civil War"

not "Conrad" **or even** "Conrad's *Heart of Darkness*" **but** "Animal Imagery in *Heart of Darkness*"

Simply to refine your topic, however, is not enough. You must make it clear to your reader that you have something to say about that topic, a point or **thesis.** You must analyze your subject critically, not just describe it. Never simply talk about abolitionist tracts without showing **how** they may have led to the Civil War; never just give examples of Conrad's animal images without also discussing **why** he uses them. Papers should never be written only to show that you have read something. They must show the result of your thinking and questions about what you have read.

Make sure that you have a thesis, rather than just a topic. Think of your paper as an experiment, in which you see if your analysis supports an hypothesis that you've stated at the beginning. The following could be **hypotheses** (sometimes called **thesis statements**):

Abolitionist tracts, though often sentimental or theoretical, did lead to the Civil War.

Conrad uses animal imagery for even the best of his characters to show the hypocrisy of European civilization.

Another way to make sure you have a thesis is to force yourself to write a sentence about your paper that follows this form: **Although** such and such, **nevertheless** so and so is true, **because:** reason one, reason two, reason three. . . .

Although *critics have recently argued that Abolitionist tracts had few practical effects,* **nevertheless** *two tracts did lead directly to the Civil War,* **because** . . .

Although *Conrad rarely criticizes European civilization directly,* **nevertheless** *his animal imagery shows the hypocrisy of its civilized facades,* **be-**

cause . . . (or, in this case, *as we can see in the following examples*).

This formula will lead to a clumsy sentence that you should not use in your papers. But it will give you a provisional outline: the **although** section in the first paragraph, the **nevertheless** section in the second (these two can also be reversed), then a paragraph or two for each of your **becauses.** It will also guarantee that you have something to say, that you have considered some arguments against your position, and that you have some reasons for it. Later, as you edit and revise your paper, you will probably find it necessary to make this outline more varied or more subtle — or perhaps to abandon it altogether. The thinking involved in constructing that clumsy sentence, however, is never wasted: you have defined your thesis.

C.   Structuring a paper; carrying on an argument

A good paper moves steadily toward a goal. Every paragraph and every idea in it should be clearly related to that goal. Cut out peripheral facts and ideas, no matter how fascinating. Cut out plot summaries, descriptions, or discussions of previous research that do not contribute to your argument.

1. Methods of argument. Your papers will move toward their goals in different ways, depending on your topic. For each paper you will need to choose a different strategy or combination of strategies, but be sure that you choose your strategy instead of letting it choose you. In each paper you will define, analyze, explain, compare, evaluate, or use some mixture of these and other techniques.

Reconsider your strategy when you have written your first draft: What method or methods have I used here? What other methods could I have used instead? Is this comparison relevant? How does this analysis support my point? What would change in my paper if I used another strategy, and would the change be an improvement?

2. *Order of argument.* You will also find that each paper demands a different order. Some papers — particularly descriptions of processes, personal experiences, narrative history — can be organized chronologically, in sequential order. (Be sure, though, that you don't simply follow the order of a work you're analyzing when another arrangement would bring out your points more effectively. Beware of simple plot summary or empty paraphrase.)

Some papers — particularly papers in which you are proving an assertion you made at the beginning — can best be organized in order of difficulty. Put the simplest and most obvious point first, and move toward the most complex and interesting one. This helps your reader grasp your argument gradually, and it helps you avoid anticlimax.

Comparison and contrast papers are perhaps the most often assigned — and the most often muddled. As in any paper, you must have a purpose; never just compare for the sake of comparing, but to show something about your subjects.

Your purpose should help you decide on your organization. For some purposes, a **point-to-point** organization would be best. You might begin, for example, with a discussion of the ways in which your subjects are alike, then move on to a discussion of the ways in which they differ. This order would be most effective if you are trying to establish the differences between two things that initially seemed alike. Reverse the order if you are trying to establish likenesses between two things that initially seemed quite different. (Be careful to keep your purpose in mind; don't get so lost in minute comparisons that you lose sight of the whole.)

Some comparison and contrast papers, on the other hand, work best with a **chunk-to-chunk** method. First, discuss one of the things you are comparing completely; then discuss the other, in the same order, constantly referring to the first. Remember that you must treat the same subjects in the same order, though they need not get equal time. This method works best when one of your subjects is less important or less interesting than the other; you can get it out of the way quickly and concentrate on the second one. (Be careful, however, to remember to compare and to swing back to your first subject at least briefly at the end.)

Again, you will often want to combine and vary these orders and methods. And again you should question your organization as you revise your first draft.

3. Logic of argument. Good papers depend on good reasoning. You must be sure that you have examined your underlying assumptions and made them clear to your reader. Precise thinking in any discipline demands that your basic assumptions be as explicit as possible and that you don't contradict these assumptions anywhere in your paper. You must also be sure that your ideas follow each other logically, that you have given sufficient evidence or proof for your arguments, that you have acknowledged important conflicting opinions or contradictory facts and dealt with them. (Writing an **although, nevertheless, because** sentence like the ones described on pages 4 and 5 will help you check the last two.)

As you write your paper, ask yourself what makes you find your thesis convincing. Then ask if you have given the reader a chance to check its validity. Your reader must be able to follow the logical steps you have made and to examine the evidence you have relied on. Test your generalizations by thinking of exceptions and counter-arguments. Be sure that you are being logical when you claim to be logical; don't sprinkle *hence, therefore,* and *thus* where no logical relationship exists.

When you have finished a first draft and it has had a chance to cool, re-read it as objectively and as critically as possible. Would you, as a detached or even hostile reader, understand the connections between your thesis, supporting evidence, and conclusions? Would you understand the important terms, or should they be defined? Would you find the treatment fair, or have objections and troubling evidence been swept under the rug? Be the first and fiercest critic of your own logic.

4. Coherence of argument. Your paper must be coherent. Each sentence, each paragraph, each idea must be firmly linked to what precedes and follows it; your reader must be able to see what connects one step of your argument to the next. Sometimes the connection will be apparent without any specific linking

device. Sometimes, however, you will need to give your reader a signal to show exactly what the connection is. You can signal by using transitional words or phrases:

> **To show addition:** *also, further, likewise, moreover, and*
>
> **To show likeness:** *similarly, likewise, in the same way*
>
> **To show contrast:** *however, even so, still, nevertheless, but, on the other hand, while*
>
> **To give an example:** *for instance, in particular, for example*
>
> **To sum up:** *finally, in short, briefly*
>
> **To conclude:** *therefore, thus, hence, accordingly*

Compare the following, first without and then with transitional signals:

> *Most trios have a circular tri-partite organization: ABA. This trio is cumulative: ABC. The C section is closer to the A than to the B section. It is not just a variation.*

> *Most trios have a circular tri-partite organization: ABA. This trio,* **however** *is cumulative,* **not circular:** *ABC. The C section is closer to the A than to the B section,* **but** *it is not just a variation.*

If over-used, however, these signals can become wooden and plodding. Short connectives are often more economical and less clumsy than long ones; try substituting *but* or *yet* for *however*, for example. Use the simplest form that will do the job. Often you can link two sentences more smoothly by repeating a word or words:

> *Your reader must be able to see what* **connects** *one step of your argument to the next. Sometimes the* **connection** *will be apparent without any specific linking devices.*

or by shifting to a pronoun with a clear antecedent:

> *The helix cannot be superposed on its mirror*

> *image.* **It** *has two distinct forms, right-handed and*
> *left-handed.*

or by adding a word like *this* or *these:*

> *Many stunts and magic tricks illustrate the princi-*
> *ples of symmetry and asymmetry. One of the best of*
> **these** *tricks makes use of a package of Camel*
> *cigarettes.*

You can make sure that your sentences and paragraphs hold together by underlining linking words and phrases in an early draft of your paper. But sometimes, after your paper is finished, you will discover that you can eliminate some mechanical connectives like *therefore, however,* or *thus,* since the direction of your argument has become clear without them. Use connectives where they will do the most good; don't use them as an impressive decoration where they are unnecessary. Like all other techniques of organization, they should simply help your reader understand your argument.

D. Beginning and ending

The most difficult parts of a paper for most students are the beginning and the ending. Too often the first and last paragraphs are nearly identical, the last paragraph merely a restatement or paraphrase of the first. Too often they reveal that the paper has no thesis, sometimes even that it has no topic.

Remember the useful advice the King in *Alice in Wonderland* gives the White Rabbit:

> *The White Rabbit put on his spectacles. "Where shall I*
> *begin, please your Majesty?" he asked.*
> *"Begin at the beginning," the King said gravely,*
> *"and go on till you come to the end; then stop."*

Many papers begin sentences or even paragraphs before the real beginning, and either stop abruptly somewhere before the end or go on for quite a while after it. Sometimes students are misled by old formulae: the funnel or hourglass technique, movement from general to specific to general again, or that old recipe for a boring paper — "You tell them what you're going to tell them, then you tell them, then you tell them what you told them." Try to move beyond those formulae to find the right form for each particular paper.

1. Beginning. How can you tell where your paper should begin? What should a first paragraph do? Certainly by the end of the first paragraph — or first sentences in a very short paper, first paragraphs in a longer one — your reader should have some idea what you are planning to show in that paper, what your thesis is. (See "Refining your topic; defining your thesis," p. 3, for a discussion of thesis or point.)

Your first paragraph should establish the tone and attitude you plan to take throughout the rest of the paper. If your first paragraph is stiff and wooden, your reader will fear that the rest of your paper will be too. Make your reader care about what you're doing. Your first paragraph is your chance to catch your reader's attention, to make your reader start thinking with you.

A beginning that is grandiose or pretentious makes your reader immediately suspicious and irritable. Avoid what is sometimes called the "as ages roll" paragraph, a paragraph that moves grandly from the beginning of recorded history to your specific problem. Avoid similar generalizations that you will never have space or time enough to prove, that would really require a book (or a life-work). Such beginnings just undermine your reader's faith in your reasoning.

> *All artists everywhere, in every time and culture,*
> *have been obsessed with the problem of self.*

Don't sprinkle in background information that any reader of your paper would be likely to know already:

> *In his fourth-century BC dialogue known as the*
> Symposium, *the Greek philosopher Plato, a stu-*
> *dent of Socrates, examines Socrates' theory of*
> *love.*
>
> This is overkill. Try: *In the* Symposium *Plato exam-*
> *ines Socrates' theory of love.*

Avoid these zoom-lens openings; focus on your specific subject as quickly as possible.

Too many first paragraphs just mark time. The following sentence illustrates the problem in miniature:

> *While it seems clear that the two books are not*
> *entirely homogeneous in nature, it seems to be*
> *equally clear, if not indeed a more pertinent*
> *observation, that Fielding has used Cervantes as*
> *a model for his work.*

This sentence finally gets around to saying something in the last ten words; everything before them is so cautious as to be almost meaningless. Notice that the first thirty-odd words could introduce **any** comparison of **any** two books. Avoid such interchangeable parts. Again, be specific about your subject right away. After finishing your paper, look back to see how far down from the beginning you can cut it.

Your first sentence does not always have to be your "thesis statement." Some writers start with a provocative quotation, a startling fact, a pointed question. Some start with an interesting example or even a telling joke. You can lead into your thesis gradually and engagingly by beginning with something specific that suggests why you chose your subject.

Remember, too, that your first paragraph need not be written first. You will, of course, have some sort of working beginning, a hypothesis, or a question you're trying to answer. But often as you begin writing the rest of your paper, you will hit your stride, find a more appropriate tone or vocabulary, discover a particularly good example. You can then go back to recast your first paragraph, using your discoveries to introduce your reader to your subject in the cleanest and most effective way.

2. Ending. Your last paragraph should never simply echo your first. If you find yourself restating your first paragraph when you begin writing your last one, **stop.** Go back to your first paragraph to see if you can rewrite it to make it suggestive rather than conclusive. Sometimes you can pose a question in the first paragraph that you then answer fully in the last one; sometimes you can give an example or illustration or quotation in the first paragraph that you can reintroduce or refer to at the end to show your reader how much better she understands it now. Sometimes you will find that you should simply move your original first paragraph to the end.

If your last paragraph is merely an echo, your reader will suspect that your paper has not gotten anywhere. Ask yourself what you have learned while writing it, what you now know or see more clearly than you did when you sketched your first paragraph. Your last paragraph is your last chance to frame your essential ideas in a succinct and convincing way, to pull together the strands of your argument, to draw conclusions, to suggest their implications. Avoid *thus we see that* . . .; just say what you hope your reader sees. You may find an example or a quotation or a fascinating fact that seems to sum up all that you've been saying; save it for your last paragraph. Be sure that your last sentence is both forceful and interesting; end with a bang, not a whimper. Conclusions should both pull together what has gone before and round off your paper — or, to echo the King's advice to the White Rabbit, conclusions should conclude.

E.   Answering essay questions

Essay questions give you a limited time to sort out and pull together what you know. Sometimes you're simply asked to write a coherent essay about a given topic, with evidence from two or three different texts. Sometimes you're asked to compare and contrast two pictures, two poems, two ideas. Often you must agree or disagree with a given statement. How do you go about answering questions like these? What is the best strategy?

Answering essay questions is different from writing papers, of course. You must keep one eye on the clock. Allot yourself a certain amount of time for each question and stick to it; leave some space after each answer so that you can expand it if you have time later. You usually won't have the texts to check quotations. (A paraphrase or summary of passages from the text will always do, though you should introduce key words when you can and define them if necessary.) You will probably have only a few minutes to jot down an outline for your answer, but be sure to make one, however sketchy, so that you won't forget an important point as the clock ticks away.

In spite of these differences, the suggestions we have made above for writing papers apply to essay exams in a condensed and urgent way. In essay answers, as in papers, you must have a **thesis.** An answer that simply juxtaposes examples from or analyses of different sources is never satisfactory. Don't just tell what Rousseau and Locke each said about liberty, but compare their statements and definitions to show where they disagree (or even perhaps agree). Don't just list examples of different kinds of love in the *Iliad* and in the *Divine Comedy*, but compare them to show the differences in the writers' conceptions of love. You must have an **argument,** a position that you are trying to defend.

Essay answers, like papers, must be **coherent.** Don't tell all you know; include only what is relevant for the question. Plot summary, lengthy discussion of minor points, rehashing of class discussion or peripheral lecture material will never help you answer a question. Decide what evidence is crucial for a good answer to a specific question, and give only that evidence.

Essay answers, like papers, must begin and end with material that is both relevant and fresh. Be sure to state your thesis at or near the beginning, so that your reader — probably rushed — will see immediately that you are making a point. Be sure to end with a statement or an example that ties your argument together; don't simply drift off or stop. (The absence of a conclusion always gives the impression that you've planned your time badly or don't have much to say, often both.)

Essay exams, like papers, require you to reason about what you have read, not simply memorize details or parrot pat solutions. The kind of reasoning you should do is the kind of reasoning that is useful any time. Suppose someone asks you, "Do you think Northampton or Holyoke is a nicer city?" You could give a world almanac description of each city — population, area, industry, climate, sociology — and then lean back and say, "That's why I like Northampton (or Holyoke) better." You haven't answered the question, but simply given a lot of detail —any that might have been relevant buried under all that isn't. Or you could say, "I like Northampton very much for the following reasons, but I also like Holyoke for these reasons." Here you have just juxtaposed the two towns. Even if you have some carefully selected detail, you have no comparison, no argument, and no thesis. Your questioner wants an evaluation, not an evasion. Again you haven't answered the question.

To answer it, you would have to say something like "I think Northampton is a nicer city, because by *nice* I mean quiet and green. I have statistics, impressions, quotations to show that there's more open space, less traffic, and less industrial noise in Northampton than in Holyoke." That's an answer: it states the problem and the grounds on which you're going to consider it, defines terms (what do you mean by *nice*?), gives your conclusion and evidence that supports that particular conclusion. It neither attempts to overwhelm the reader with piles of undifferentiated detail, nor waffles.

When answering an essay question, you should go through each of these steps:

1. **Before writing:** Decide how long you have for the question. As you think about it, jot down examples to use later. Sketch an outline for your answer, or write an **although, nevertheless, because** sentence, to refer to while you're writing.

2. **While writing:** Begin with a statement of your thesis. Indicate what is problematic about the question, why pat answers won't do. Then reason about the problem, defining terms and giving carefully chosen, relevant evidence and examples. Conclude, very briefly, by showing what you've proved.

3. **After writing:** Reread your answer carefully. Check your argument, your definitions, the relevance of your examples. Check for missing words or sentences. Cross out and rewrite any word that might possibly be illegible; don't expect your reader to be a cryptographer. (If you know your writing is hard to read, write on **every other** line.)

A good essay answer shows grace under pressure. It is concise, precise, and to the point.

II. Choosing the Right Words

Mark Twain once said that the difference between the right word and the wrong word is like the difference between lightning and a lightning bug. But how do you find the right one, tell the flash from the flicker?

Your first guide, of course, is a good dictionary, a dictionary that gives derivations, examples, and synonyms: *The American Heritage Dictionary*, New College Edition; *Webster's New Collegiate Dictionary*, Revised Edition; *The Random House Collegiate Dictionary*, for example. Use your dictionary to check your word choice, to see if a near-synonym might be closer to what you mean, to see if the word has a metaphorical basis or connotations that undercut your idea, to check spelling or the preposition used with a word. Keep a good, solid, hard-bound dictionary handy whenever you're writing, and use it.

You also should become familiar with the two-volume *Compact Edition of the Oxford English Dictionary*, often called simply and affectionately the *OED*. Like other Oxford dictionaries, the *OED* gives British rather than American usage; it also lacks words that have become current since 1933; the print is very small and hard to read without a magnifying glass. But even with these limitations, it remains the most inclusive and incisive guide to the changing meanings of English words.

Fowler's *Modern English Usage*, Second Edition, should be next to your dictionaries. Like the *OED*, it reflects British, not American, spellings and practice; but it is the most valuable example we have of thinking about choices among words: witty, precise, full of funny examples. The American quasi-equivalents (Roy Copperud's *American Usage: The Consensus* or Theodore Bernstein's *Watch Your Language*, for example) are often useful, but less clear and less convincing.

We can also recommend several inexpensive paperbacks that we have found helpful in writing this handbook, books that consider the problem of word choice in a larger context: *The*

Elements of Style, by William Strunk, Jr., and E.B. White (sections IV and V in particular); *Revising Prose*, by Richard A. Lanham; *The Reader Over Your Shoulder*, by Robert Graves and Alan Hodge (again British, but good). They all show ways to pare your prose down, to cut the flab and fog out of your writing. George Orwell, in his essay "Politics and the English Language," does this as part of his campaign against the misuse of language for political purposes. To write well, you must take language seriously. These books will help you begin looking **at** it, instead of only **through** it.

Though your skill in choosing words and looking at your own language will develop only as you read and practice, we can give you a few general guidelines for word choice in your papers. (Notice that these are guidelines, not straitjackets.)

A. Everyday, not fancy, words

Many students believe that papers should be written in a special language, a language much more abstract, elaborate, and remote than the language they would use in a letter. This is not true. Though slang is seldom appropriate and though you will sometimes need to use the special vocabulary of a discipline, you should stay as close as possible to the words you use every day. Compare, for example, the simple proverb

> *People who live in glass houses shouldn't throw stones.*

with Chaytor's inflated version of it:

> *Individuals normally resident in dwelling houses constructed wholly or mainly of glass or other vitreous substances should be careful to remember the potential repercussion consequent upon lapidary projection.*

What distinguishes these two sentences? The second, elaborate one is three times as long, 28 words as opposed to 9. It is full of weak qualifying words and phrases and unnecessary adjectives: "*normally* resident," "*wholly or mainly of* glass *or other vitreous substances*," "*dwelling* houses." (What other kind of house could you be "resident in"?) The second one also is full of long words derived from Latin: "individuals" instead of "people," "resident in" instead of "live," "vitreous substances" in addition to "glass," "lapidary projection" instead of "throwing stones," with a few just thrown in: "potential," "repercussion," "consequent." The long Latinate version obscures the point of the pithy proverb.

In general you should rely on short, concrete words, using longer, more abstract words only when necessary. Choosing the simpler word often forces you to say, or to discover, exactly what you mean. It may also force you into conflict with American Officialese, the bureaucratic or institutional style, the style of Dickens' Circumlocution Office. Official, particularly government, prose delights in inflated language:

> *This reorganization of material is designed to facilitate the optimal utilization of the system's capability.*

Rough translation: *We've moved things around so they'll be easier to use.*

In a country full of *adjusters of delinquent obligations* and *domestic engineers*, it takes some courage to say *bill-collectors* and *housewives* (or *househusbands*). You may have to ask for *decorator ebony* to get the black phone you want, but in your own writing avoid this pompous, windy style. Keep it simple.

Rule of thumb: Avoid long nouns that end in *-tion* and *-ity*, adjectives that end in *-tional*, verbs that end in *-ate* and *-ize*.

Never use a complex or fancy word where a simpler one will do:

use, **not** *employ* or *utilize*
show, **not** *exemplify, demonstrate, exhibit*, or *expose*
help, **not** *facilitate*
say, **not** *assert, asseverate, proclaim, expound*, or *declare*
has, **not** *possess*

B.   Active, not passive, constructions

A simple sentence in English usually goes like this:

The dog bit the man.

This sentence is in the active voice; the subject of the sentence (the dog) is doing the biting. We can, however, turn it around:

The man was bitten by the dog.

This sentence is in the passive voice; the subject of the sentence (the man this time) is no longer doing the biting, but being bitten. The action is no longer direct, but indirect. The verb is no longer simple but compound, the verb *to be* plus a past participle *(bitten)*.

Occasionally the passive voice can be useful and even effective. Use it when you want to emphasize frailty or inertness:

The old man was led from the burning house.

The rudderless ship had been tossed for days on the stormy sea.

Use the passive voice when you want to maintain your focus on a subject that is sometimes the doer, sometimes the done-to:

Lincoln fought long and hard in all his campaigns. Although he was defeated by Stephen A. Douglas in the 1858 election for the Senate, he immediately began preparations for the Republican Presidential Convention in 1860.

But usually you should keep your sentences direct, in the active voice. The passive voice permits you to evade responsibility for your opinions and ideas: *it can be seen that, it can be shown that, it has been decided that.* In every case we can ask, "By whom?" (Politicians love the passive voice, since it permits them to say something *must be done* without specifying who will do it, or to say *it was decided* without saying who made the decision. Think of President Ford commenting on the pardon he gave ex-President Nixon: "When the pardon was given . . . ")

Look at the following sentences, all from students' papers:

Hareton was shaped into Heathcliff's image.
This is quite concise, but imprecise. By reversing it we can show exactly who did the shaping: *Heathcliff shaped Hareton in his own image.*

Societal conditioning is established by developing contingencies of reinforcement that are relative to accepted norms of behavior.
The passive voice here makes the windy language even windier. We think this means something like *Reinforcement establishes socially acceptable behavior.*

Rule of Thumb: Avoid the verb *to be (is, are, was, were,* etc.) whenever possible. Scratch other weak verbs like *seems* and *exists* from your list, too, while you're at it.

Don't be afraid to say *I.* Students sometimes use the passive voice because they have been taught to avoid using *I.* But *I* is now perfectly acceptable in any scholarly writing, even the most technical, as long as your emphasis is on the text, the facts, or the experiment, rather than on your reactions and feelings. In scientific writing, you can use the first person and the active voice without shifting the focus from the operations and results to the experimenter.

Not *It was observed that,* **but** *I observed*
Not *This analysis can be interpreted to show,* **but** *I have shown* or *this analysis shows*
Not *Though Smith has argued this way, it can be argued that,* **but** *Though Smith has argued this way, I believe that*

I is not taboo. Attempts to avoid *I* have made prose more and more bloodless and impersonal.

C.   Lean, not flabby, prose

Say it the shortest way. Because people are insensitive to language, they tend to crank sentences out like sausages, link by link, or like "sections of a prefabricated henhouse," as Orwell said. Think back to the two sentences about glass houses on p. 16 and then look at the following examples, again from students' papers:

1. *Another line of definition can be drawn by way of comparing the two men in the way they both perceive certain situations.* (22 words)

2. *This paragraph provides a vehicle for the writer to create a distinct separation between the two sections.* (17 words)

3. *In the two novels, each author employs the use of setting as a tool to forebode incidents and allude to the past.* (22 words)

What has gone wrong? These writers are not listening to themselves. (Clumps of words almost next to each other, like *employ the use* or *by way of* and *in the way*, suggest this.) It's even possible that they're not thinking about the words they're using. (You can't use a vehicle to create, or a tool to forebode.) All of them are using language automatically, or letting language use them. The first example is the only one in the passive voice, but in all three cases the writer seems afraid to let anything act directly. (The paragraph *provides a vehicle for the writer to;* the authors *employ the use of setting to. . . .)*

If we **listen, think,** and **ask where the action really is,** we might come up with the following revisions, each about half as long as the original:

1. *The two men also perceive the same situations differently.* (9 words)

2. *This paragraph separates the two sections.* (6 words)

3. *In both novels, setting foreshadows the future and alludes to the past.* (12 words) (A look at a good dictionary would have prevented the misuse of *forebode.* And *the future* provides a better contrast with *the past* than the vaguer *incidents.)*

Richard Lanham's *Revising Prose* can be a great help here.

Some sentence beginnings always send the word-count shooting up. Avoid them:

> *There is, there are, there was, there were*
> *He is a man who*
> *It is . . . who, it is . . . that*
> *The fact of the matter is that, the fact is, the truth is*
> *The nature of the case is that*

(Notice that all of them involve the verb *to be,* which you should be avoiding anyway.) *There is* and its relatives are particularly foggy because they permit you to string a sentence together without a lively verb:

> 4. *There are many connections between what is*
>   *happening inside a room and outside the win-*
>   *dow.* (15 words)

> 5. *There is a clear comparison in these shields.*
>   *There is also a contrast in the shields, not only in*
>   *their content but also in their relationship to*
>   *their beholders.* (29 words)

These sentences are difficult to revise precisely because they are so vague. What connections? What comparisons? What contrasts? What is really happening in these sentences, or what should be happening? Again, if you **listen, think,** and **ask where the action really is,** you might come up with something like these:

> 4. *What happens outside the window* (the
>   weather?) *corresponds to what happens inside.*
>   *(*10, or 7, words)

But perhaps what she really means is *Weather reflects events in the plot.*

> 5. *Though alike in form, the shields show different*
>   *events and have different effects on their*
>   *beholders.* (16 words)

Certain words and phrases also inflate or deaden prose. Avoid them, too:

*the fact that (*See Strunk and White, p. xiv and
   p. 24)
because of
of a . . . nature (of a serious nature = serious)
of a . . . basis (on a daily basis = daily or *every*
   day)
factor, aspect, vehicle, facet, element (except in
   chemistry)

As Ezra Pound once said, "Incompetence will show in the use of
too many words." Be ruthless about getting rid of words that are
useless or just going along for the ride.

D. Dangerous words

The following words occur frequently in students' papers,
often in the wrong places. In most cases, they sound deceptively
similar. The next time you plan to use one, look it up.

affect, effect   *incident, incidence*
allude, elude   *lie, lay*
allusion, illusion, elision *like, as*
ambiguous, ambivalent   *principal, principle*
assure, ensure, insure   *prophecy, prophesy*
blatant, obvious   *simple, simplistic*
complement, compliment   *social, societal*
discrete, discreet   *subordinate, sublimate*
imminent, immanent,   *transitory, transient,*
   eminent   *transitional*
imply, infer

Certain Greek and Latin words commonly used in English that
end in *a* are plural: *data, media, phenomena, criteria, spectra,
colloquia,* etc. They take plural verbs.

The *datum* is confusing; the *data* are confusing.

The *medium* is the message; the *media* give con-
   flicting messages.

The only *criterion* is excellence; the *criteria* are
   excellence and enthusiasm.

Don't invent nouns by adding endings to verbs or adjectives. Check first to see if there's an established, more streamlined noun just waiting to be used. We've recently run across:

satirization for *satire*
analyzation for *analysis*
scrutinization for *scrutiny*
structuralization for *structure*
aggressivity for *aggression*
summarization for *summary*

E.   Clichés, mixed metaphors, and jargon

In typesetting, a **cliché** was a mold used to cast metal into letters, a shape repeated over and over again. Clichés now are also combinations of words that have been repeated so often in the same shape that they have lost their force. Don't use combinations you have heard before. Though *leave no stone unturned* was probably once a vivid way to describe laborious and thorough effort, it now seems limp and unimaginative. Beware of combinations you can complete without thinking: *loud and clear, hue and cry, rack and ruin, at that point in time, fear and trembling*, to give only a few examples. You can't improve or redeem clichés by putting them in apologetic quotation marks, either; just leave them out.

Be careful not to **mix metaphors.** Sometimes people scramble them in an attempt to appeal to the senses, to make their writing more exciting: *The Senator would lead the country to the brink of war with his head in the sand.* More often, however, people mix metaphors because they are not conscious of the metaphorical bases of words they use. (Fowler calls these "battles of dead metaphors.") These occur often in combinations like: *this illustrates the void in his life* (can you really illustrate a void?), *her departure entrenches his isolation* (can you imagine a departure digging trenches around an isolation?), *the center of the issue revolves around his statement* (can you put the core around the apple?). Dead or dying metaphors can spring to life when you least expect or want them to. Think about the pictures latent in the words you use; take them literally or visualize them before you write something like *He entered the wilderness, where the hand of man had never set foot.*

Jargon, sometimes called gobbledygook, is a special problem. All disciplines have their own technical terms, words that convey complicated ideas in condensed and precise form. Where would musicians be without *rubato, pizzicato,* and *andante;* biologists without *protozoon, phylum,* and *stamen;* photographers without *lens, aperture,* and *f-stop?* If you are writing in any of these disciplines, these words will save you and your readers time. (Ask a musician to define *rubato,* for example, and see how long it takes.)

Jargon, in contrast, surrounds ideas with a mumbo-jumbo of mysterious and impressive phrases to exclude the uninitiate. Social scientists are notorious for saying simple things in a complex way: *The nature of the disintegration of instable systems of social interaction, that is, of the loss of social structure, thus focuses on the disintegration of the motivation of actors with normative cultural standards.* And we often see reflections of their jargon in the language of popular psychology: *The nature of the lifestyle they achieved was that of a meaningful relationship or togetherness in which neither intruded on the other's space.* But every discipline has its masters of gobbledygook: *His decipherment of the negative valuation of writing within the speech-writing hierarchy shows the mark of an old interpretive genealogy.* Jargon is often unintentionally funny; it is always deliberately exclusive. Use technical terms when you must, for precision and conciseness, but write for an intelligent lay audience. Don't shut it out by using a hermetic jargon; make everything as simple and as clear as you possibly can.

III. Writing Correctly

Good writing depends in part on good sentences, sentences where design reinforces meaning. Punctuation marks act as traffic signs; they help your reader negotiate your sentences easily, without wrong turns or shifts into reverse. If you construct misleading sentences or let your commas fall where they may, your reader will be at best irritated, at worst lost. "Correctness" is not just a schoolmarm's virtue; it makes your writing easier to read.

This section is certainly not a guide to all the twists and turns of English syntax, grammar, and punctuation; we've included only those problems that recur most persistently in students' papers. You can find a more complete guide to punctuation in most good dictionaries. If our discussion of other matters doesn't cover a problem you know you have, get a basic writing handbook like one of the following and use it carefully:

> Wilma R. Ebbitt and David R. Ebbitt. *Writer's Guide and Index to English.* (Scott, Foresman)

> Glenn Leggett, C. David Mead, and William Charvat. *Prentice-Hall Handbook for Writers.* (Prentice-Hall)

A. Sentence structure (syntax)

1. Dangling and misplaced modifiers. A *dangling modifier* is a sentence part, usually a phrase or clause, that modifies no word or the wrong word in a sentence.

> *By using descriptive passages, the reader gets a complete image.*

> The reader is not using the descriptive passages.
> **TRY** *The descriptive passages give the reader a complete image* OR *The writer's descriptive passages give the reader a complete image.*

> *Warm and balmy, Cathy sits at the window, fading away in the midst of a season of renewal.*

> Cathy is not balmy or warm; the weather is. **TRY** *On a warm and balmy day, Cathy sits . . . .*
>
> *Hopefully the snow will come soon.*
>
> Who is hoping? It cannot be the snow. **TRY** *I hope the snow will come soon.*
>
> *A declared misogynist, Jacob's goal was to avoid contact with women.*
>
> Here the word that follows the beginning phrase is a possessive and cannot be the subject of the sentence. **TRY** *A declared misogynist, Jacob tried to avoid . . . .*

A *misplaced modifier* is a sentence part that occurs in the wrong position.

> *FOR SALE: Mahogany table by a lady with Chippendale legs.* The table has Chippendale legs, not the lady. **TRY** *FOR SALE: Mahogany table with Chippendale legs.*
>
> *Look elsewhere for examples in this handbook of poorly constructed sentences.*
>
> This is not (hopefully!) a handbook full of poorly constructed sentences. **TRY** *Look elsewhere in this handbook for examples of poorly constructed sentences.*
>
> *In San Diego, the "in" place for years has been McDini's for corned beef. Thinly sliced and heaped on rye, corned beef lovers won't be disappointed.*
>
> They'll be in a lot of pain, though, as the *New Yorker* said . . . . *McDini's for corned beef, thinly sliced and heaped on rye. Corned beef lovers won't be disappointed.*

The most knock-kneed sentences begin with a dangling modifier and continue with a weak passive construction. They collapse at the joint because no subject connects the beginning with the ending.

> *By analyzing the first document, it can be seen that . . .*

Who or what is doing the analysis? **Try** *The first document shows that . . .*

> *In doing so, his strength and his honor are upheld.*

His strength and honor aren't doing anything. **Try** *His action reveals his strength and his honor.*

Careless writers often scatter *which*-clauses here and there without making clear exactly what they refer to.

> *After his stormy childhood, he was unable to take advice from his uncles when he became king, which was very unfortunate.*

What was unfortunate, that he became king, that he couldn't take advice, that his childhood was stormy? Rephrase and restructure: *Unfortunately, his stormy childhood made him unable to accept advice from his uncles when he became king.*

"Trying to cross a paragraph by leaping from *which* to *which* is like Eliza crossing the ice," as James Thurber said. Make sure that your *whiches* do not refer to a conglomeration of possibilities. Anchor them firmly to a specific antecedent. (Watch similar loose *thises*, too.)

2. Parallelism.

Parts of a sentence that are parallel in thought and function should also be parallel in form. Notice what happens when we omit the parallelism in the preceding sentence:

> *Parts of a sentence that are parallel in thought and function should also be similar when it comes to form.*

In our first and better version, the repetition of *parallel* and the similar construction of *in thought and function* and *in form* underline the logical connections the sentence is making. Without such repetitions and constructions, your reader won't see which parts of your sentence are linked.

Repeat as many words as possible in parallel construction to emphasize the crucial differences. This technique is one source of the power of many nursery rhymes:

> **Compare** *Jack Sprat could eat no fat; his wife,*
> *however, could not digest the more muscular*
> *parts of the animal* **with** *Jack Sprat could eat no*
> *fat. His wife could eat no lean.*

of good political speeches:

> **Compare** *government that the citizens manage*
> *themselves and operated for their benefit* **with**
> *government of the people, by the people, and for*
> *the people.*

and of many passages from the Bible:

> **Compare** *The mourners are blessed, because they*
> *shall be comforted. The meek, who shall inherit*
> *the earth, are also blessed* **with** *Blessed are they*
> *that mourn: for they shall be comforted. Blessed*
> *are the meek: for they shall inherit the earth.*
> (Matthew v, 4-5)

When you give a series or a list, all the items in the series must have the same grammatical form, be constructed in the same way:

> *A villain is usually dashing, courageous, appears*
> *to be wealthy, and in general a charmer.*

> All of these should be adjectives. *A villain is usu-*
> *ally dashing, courageous, apparently wealthy,*
> *and charming.*

Certain pairs of words require parallel construction: *both/ and, either/or, neither/nor, not only/but also.* Be sure that you place these pairs just before the parts of the sentence you mean to connect:

> *She refuses to go either to the store or to stay home.*
> **Try** *She refuses either to go to the store or to stay*
> *home.*

*He wants not only to live in the country but also by
    the sea.*

Here *to live* introduces both of the phrases, so you
    must put *not only* after it: *He wants to live not
    only in the country but also by the sea.*

3. Coordination, subordination, and emphasis.

Occasionally, inexperienced writers produce a series of short,
choppy sentences, in beginning-reader style:

*Patroclus represented Achilles. Patroclus was tak-
    ing Achilles' place in the fighting. Patroclus was
    wearing Achilles' armor.*

This choppy writing not only sounds childish but also makes it
impossible for your reader to tell which idea is most important,
where you want your emphasis to fall. Design your sentences to
indicate the relative importance of your ideas and their connections:

*Patroclus represented Achilles by taking his place
    in the fighting and wearing his armor.*

When two ideas are of equal importance, link them with a coor-
dinating conjunction *(and, or, but, yet, for, nor)*. Note that the
comma comes before, not after, such conjunctions:

You take the high road, and I'll take the low road.

*Patroclus took Achilles' place in the fighting, but
    Achilles stayed near the hollow ships.*

But avoid weak *ands*. *And* is the vaguest connector we have. Do
not string loosely related ideas together with *and*. Specify the
logical connection more exactly, or separate them completely.

*We have a lot to do this morning, and my father is
    coming this afternoon.*

Revise to show the real problem: *We have to finish
    everything before my father gets here this
    afternoon.*

*In the first chapters grey fog blankets everything,
and Dickens begins to describe his characters.*

Show the connections: *In the first chapters a
blanket of grey fog obscures both London and the
characters.*

Always put the more important part of your sentence in the main clause, the less important in a subordinate clause.

*He was halfway up the mountain when a cougar
sprang out of the underbrush.*

Don't hide the cougar's spring. *When he was half
way up the mountain, a cougar sprang out of the
underbrush.*

The most interesting part of your sentence belongs at the end. Like football games and spy movies, sentences should lead up to a climax. (Paragraphs and papers should, too.) Don't let incidental ideas or afterthoughts obscure your point.

Compare *The governor is a dangerous crook, as
you all know,* **with** *The governor, as you all
know, is a dangerous crook.*

*Wrenching the crown from the hands of the Pope,
Napoleon crowned himself in Notre Dame on
December 2, 1804.*
Here the relatively unimportant prepositional
phrases at the end deaden the more interesting
parts. **Try** *On December 2, 1804, Napoleon
crowned himself in Notre Dame, wrenching the
crown from the hands of the Pope.*

Try to vary your sentence lengths, structures, and rhythms. While a series of very short sentences can be monotonous and choppy, a series of long, complex sentences can be monotonous and soporific. Include an occasional short sentence or question to wake your reader up.

*As we were walking down the shady lane, we saw a
snake slither into the ditch. Although we were all
very frightened, only Jane screamed. After she*

stopped screaming, we saw that Martha had fainted.

All these sentences are set up the same way and have the same rhythm. Compare this with *As we were walking down the shady lane, we saw a snake slither into the ditch. Jane screamed. Only as she stopped screaming did we realize that Martha had fainted.*

B.   Punctuation

1. Incomplete sentences.   To punctuate sentences correctly, you must understand the difference between **main** or **independent** (grammatically complete) and **subordinate** or **dependent** (grammatically incomplete) clauses. An independent clause, since it is complete in itself, may stand alone as a sentence:

We were eating chocolate.

A phrase or dependent clause, since it is not complete in itself, may not stand alone:

While we were eating chocolate . . .
Because we were eating chocolate . . .
Eating many different kinds of chocolate . . .

Incomplete sentences or sentence fragments that occur in students' papers are usually fairly complex. Sometimes a participial phrase (a phrase introduced by a word ending in *-ing* or *-ed)* drifts, not just dangles, without any grammatical anchor:

The article was full of factual errors, but still useful. Treating the causes and effects of the Industrial Revolution.

The long participial phrase cannot stand alone. One of the many ways to revise this would be *Though the article was full of factual errors, it did include a useful treatment of the causes and effects of the Industrial Revolution.*

Sometimes a dependent clause, introduced by words like *while, because, whereas, although, for,* wavers alone:

> *The growth of urban centers had far-reaching con-*
> *sequences for the organization of skilled labor.*
> *Because the patriarchal management of fac-*
> *tories, possible in isolated communities, was no*
> *longer appropriate.*
> A comma instead of the period after *labor* would
> solve the problem.

Check your sentences. Make sure they are complete, that you haven't unwisely granted independence to a participial phrase or a dependent clause.

2. *Run-on sentences.*

2. *Run-on sentences.* Run-on sentences or comma faults occur when two complete sentences are fused with a comma. Sentences that involve words like *however, therefore, hence, so, also, moreover, sometimes* cause the most difficulty:

> *He was willing to go, however, he did make certain*
> *demands.*
> Here you need either a semicolon or a period after
> *go;* a comma isn't enough.

> *They did not measure the chemicals accurately,*
> *therefore, the experiment was a failure.*
> Again, you need a fuller stop before *therefore,* either
> a semicolon or a period.

3. *Commas.*

3. *Commas.* Use a comma to indicate a brief pause, a small separation. Commas separate two main clauses connected with *and, but, yet, or, nor, for;* simple items in a series; a long introductory phrase or clause and the rest of the sentence; or a parenthetical or incidental word, phrase, or clause:

> *The girls, on the other hand, were not enthusiastic.*
> *The weather, you will be amazed to hear, has been*
> *bright and sunny.*
> *John, after he had burned the toast, went on to spill*
> *the coffee.*

Parenthetical items can be tricky. Ask yourself if the sentence would be complete and make sense without the word, phrase, or clause. If it would, **enclose** the parenthetical words in commas; don't let them trickle into the rest of the sentence on one side or the other.

The same rule applies to all non-restrictive or parenthetical parts of a sentence. Many comma mistakes come from the failure to distinguish between **restrictive or defining clauses,** clauses that are necessary to identify the nouns they modify, and **non-restrictive or non-defining clauses,** clauses that give additional but not identifying information. If a clause isn't necessary for the meaning of the sentence, **enclose** it in commas. If it is, omit the commas.

> *All students, who have been cheating on their exams, will be expelled.* (Every student in the school)

> *All students who have been cheating on their exams will be expelled.* (only a few students)

> *We were eating chocolate, which was our favorite food.*

> *We were eating the chocolate that Aunt Emily sent us* (as opposed to other possible chocolates).

> *I went to find my book, which was on the table.*

> *The book that is on the table is mine; the one on the floor is yours.*

(Note that most careful writers use *that* to introduce a restrictive clause, *which* to introduce a non-restrictive clause.)

4. Semicolons. Use a semicolon to connect independent clauses that are very close in thought **if** they are **not** connected by a coordinating conjunction *(and, but, yet, or, nor, for)*.

> *A period means STOP; a semicolon means YIELD.*

> *He looked exhausted; his face was caked with ashes, sweat, and tears.*

Use semicolons to divide items in a series that already includes internal punctuation, usually commas:

> *She promised to bring her guitar, the one her brother had lent her; her extra sleeping bag, even if it was a little torn; and a big bag of marshmallows.*

5. Colons.

Use a colon to announce something to follow, as a fanfare to introduce a list, a clarification, a quotation, or a question. A colon implies that you are moving from the general to the specific or that the second part of the sentence is the result of the first.

> *Three things accounted for his success: his energy, his industry, and his grandfather's money.*

> *Her argument was clear and simple: only community action could stop the development.*

> *He repeated it over and over again: "Carthage must be destroyed."*

Note that the part of the sentence before the colon must be able to stand alone.

6. Dashes.

Use dashes to set off an afterthought or loosely connected idea from the rest of the sentence. Dashes separate more sharply than commas and are more informal than parentheses — so informal, in fact, that you should use them sparingly in your papers.

> *One writer — I think it was Keats — thought that the poet should be a chameleon.*

Separate such asides clearly from the rest of your sentence; never put a dash on one side of your afterthought, a comma on the other. Use *two* hyphens on your typewriter to create a dash.

7. Exclamation points.

Comic books and sultry novels have driven exclamation points out of serious writing. Allow yourself one a semester.

8. *Quotation marks and italics.* Put quotation marks around titles of short stories, short poems, essays, and articles: "The Jilting of Granny Weatherall," "The Solitary Reaper," "Bismarck's European Strategy," and so forth.

Italicize (<u>underline</u> on a typewriter) the titles of plays, complete books, long poems, names of ships and aircraft, scientific names (genus and species of plants and animals): *Macbeth*, *Modern English Usage, Paradise Lost, The Spirit of St. Louis, Euonymus japonicus.* You should also italicize (underline) foreign words and phrases that have not become part of the language (consult your dictionary when in doubt) and words or parts of words that you are discussing **as words:**

> The *da capo* section echoes the shift from major to minor.
> Nietzsche's *Angst* became more and more intense.
> Dictionary definitions of *genius* are inadequate.
> Menger introduced the term *marginal utility.*

9. *Hyphens.* Use a hyphen to divide a word when you run out of space at the end of a line. (Divide words as seldom as possible and never between one page and the next.) Always divide the word between syllables; check your dictionary if you're uncertain where the division falls.

> *Choco-late* or *choc-olate,* **not** *cho-colate* or *chocol-ate*

Hyphenate compound adjectives, two or more words that modify a noun not individually but as a unit.

> *grey-green eyes* (neither *grey* nor *green,* but in between)

> *half-baked theory* (neither a *half theory* nor a *baked theory,* but one only partly cooked)

When the modifier contains three terms, the hyphens are optional but should be between all the terms or none of them.

> *a low-molecular-weight compound* **or** *a low molecular weight compound*

Certain prefixes *(anti-intellectual, ex-wife, all-powerful)* and certain hybrid nouns *(philosopher-king, prison-house)* should also be hyphenated. Consult your dictionary when in doubt, since the status of hyphenated words is constantly changing.

10. Apostrophes. Use an apostrophe to form possessives. Add *'s* to all singular nouns and to plural nouns that don't end in *s*. When singular nouns end in *s*, you have the option of adding *'s* or just the apostrophe.

> *The boy's tooth*
> *Mrs. Jenkins's hat (***or*** Mrs. Jenkins' hat,* **never**
>   *Mrs. Jenkin's hat)*
> *Keats's letters (***or*** Keats' letters,* **never** *Keat's*
>   *letters)*
> *the women's room*
> *the children's toys*

Add an apostrophe **after** the *s* for plural nouns that end in *s:*

> *the boys' mouths*
> *the ladies' hats*
> *the teachers' room*

(Please don't put a sign in front of your house that says "The Snaggle's.")

Use an apostrophe to form contractions: *I'd, he'll, can't, don't, I've,* and so forth. But never use an apostrophe in a possessive pronoun. Study — memorize — the following examples:

> *Who's going in whose car? (Who's* is a contraction =
>   who is. *Whose* is a possessive pronoun.)

> *It's in its box. (It's* is a contraction = it is. *Its* is a
>   possessive pronoun.)

> *They're on their way there. (They're* is a contrac-
>   tion = they are. *Their* is a possessive pronoun.
>   *There* is an adverb indicating place.)

11. Periods. End sentences with a period, of course. Most abbreviations should also be followed by a period.

> *e.g. (exempli gratia* or for example)
> *i.e. (id est* or that is to say)
> *bull.* (bulletin)
> *cog.* (cognate)
> *sing.* (singular)

But do not use a period after the abbreviation of a unit *(g, mg, km, lb, oz, tsp)* or after most common scientific abbreviations and acronyms:

> *max* or *min* (maximum or minimum)
> *ppm* (parts per million)
> *USP* (United States Pharmacopoeia)
> *DNA* (deoxyribonucleic acid)
> *uv* (ultraviolet)

12. Capital letters. Each sentence should begin with a capital letter. This means that you should not begin a sentence with a numeral, a mathematical symbol ($\log x$), or a word that cannot begin with a capital (*o*-nitrophenol). Although the names of chemical compounds are not ordinarily capitalized, you should capitalize them at the beginning of a sentence.

Use capital letters for proper names, for the first letter of the chemical symbol for an element, for the genus (not the species) in the scientific name of a plant or animal. There are rigid rules for the capitalization of units; for guidance, see *The International System of Units SI*, NBS Special Publication No. 330 (Washington: National Bureau of Standards, 1977) or *Metric Editorial Guide*, 3rd ed. (Washington: American National Metric Council, 1978).

C. Agreement

Your verb must match the subject of the sentence in number. This agreement becomes problematic only when the subject is complicated or far removed from the verb. Don't be confused by prepositional phrases that come between the subject and the verb.

> *The comedy of the last scene and of the epilogue*
> *point up the inconsistency.*

> The subject is comedy, not *the last scene* and *the epilogue.* Therefore *The comedy of the last scene and of the epilogue points up the inconsistency.*

When you have pairs like *either/or, neither/nor*, make the verb agree with the nearer noun:

> *Neither the team nor the coaches have heard the*
> *news.*

> *Either his sisters or his mother is his greatest*
> *supporter.*

But often this rule makes your sentence sound so awkward that rewriting is the best solution.

> *Neither the players nor the coaches have heard the*
> *news.*

> *Either his parents or his sisters are his greatest*
> *supporters.*

Indefinite pronouns *(either, each, everyone, everybody, no one, someone, nobody,* and so on) are singular and take singular verbs.

> *Everyone is already there.*
> *Either of the solutions is correct.*
> *Nobody knows the trouble I've seen.*

Indefinite pronouns, unfortunately, are also followed by singular pronouns:

> *Each of the mothers brought her baby.*
> *Everybody and his little brother came.*
> *Everyone who participates in the Olympics is*
> *allowed to keep his uniform.*
> *Not one of the professors remembered to bring his*
> *book.*

Many people feel that the indefinite use of *his* is sexist and demeaning to women. After pondering various alternatives that have been suggested — the clumsy *his/her* or *her or his*, the new-fangled and ugly *ter*, the incorrect *their*, the startling *her* when both sexes are obviously meant — we can recommend only three solutions. We could continue to use *his* as a generic, not a gender, term and feel sorry for men, who have to share their pronouns with everyone else; we could use *his or her* (watching to make sure that it doesn't make our sentences too awkward); or we could systematically rewrite all such sentences:

> *A huge crowd came.*
> *All Olympic athletes are allowed to keep their*
>   *uniforms.*
> *The professors — all equally absent-minded —*
>   *forgot to bring their books.*

Don't use sex-linked pronouns *(he, her,* etc.) when you refer to animals, unless you need to specify sex. Refer to *Guidelines for Nonsexist Language in APA Journals*, Publications Change Sheet 2 (Washington: American Psychological Association, 1977).

D.   Pronoun reference

Your reader must always know exactly what noun your pronoun stands for. (Notice that *pro-noun* means *for* a noun, a substitution.) Be sure that your pronoun references are not even momentarily ambiguous:

> *Elaine told Ellen her promotion was overdue.*
> Elaine's promotion? or Ellen's? **Try** *Elaine told*
>   *Ellen, "Your promotion is overdue."*
>
> *Although good cookbooks can help beginning cooks,*
>   *they don't automatically turn out good meals.*
> The cooks? or the cookbooks? **Try** *Even with the*
>   *help of good cookbooks, beginning cooks don't*
>   *automatically turn out good meals.*

> *When your children refuse to eat more zucchini, cut*
> *them in half and bury them in the compost heap.*
> The children? or the zucchini? **Try** *Cut the zucchini*
> *in half and bury them when your children won't*
> *eat any more.* Or substitute *the squash* for *them.*

Never use the same pronoun to refer to two different things in the same sentence or consecutive sentences:

> *The Girondists insisted on their fundamental*
> *principles, but their meaning was unclear and*
> *often contradictory.*
> *Their* refers to the Girondists the first time, the
> principles the second.

> *The question of Palestine's integrity is enormously*
> *complex: before unraveling it, it would be futile*
> *to discuss it.*
> *It* refers to the question to be unravelled, then to
> the futility of the discussion, then to Palestine's
> integrity.

Avoid using a possessive noun as an antecedent; your reference will always seem unclear.

> *After the oriole's nest was destroyed, it flew away.*
> The nest? or the bird?

> *Throughout Marx's* Kapital, *he affirms that . . .*
> The *he* seems to dangle in mid-air. **Try** *Throughout*
> *the* Kapital, *Marx affirms that . . .*

Remember that, except in formulae like *it is raining*, pronouns should refer to an antecedent that your reader can locate quickly and easily. (See also the discussion of *which* and *this* on p. 27.)

E.   Tenses

Decide whether to write your paper in the present tense or the past tense, and stick to your decision. The present tense is often clearer and simpler to use. It works beautifully for discussions of events in fiction or poetry, for analysis of philosophical ideas, for conclusions in laboratory experiments, for discussion of an artist's or author's techniques, for description of processes, for anything that is not time-bound. Note that if you are writing mainly in the present tense, you need not shift very far back to express the past; use *has* not *had, was* not *had been.*

> *Although Satan was one of the foremost angels in heaven, he is now fallen and without light.*

> *The government has been volatile for years, but now it is stable.*

Never shift tenses from one paragraph to the next. Don't let quotations in a different tense make you waver. Be consistent.

IV. Referring to Your Sources

A. Why and when to document; avoiding plagiarism

When you use anyone else's words or ideas, you must acknowledge your debt. This applies to **any** borrowings: from a published work, from a lecture, or from a friend's old term paper. Failure to acknowledge your borrowings is **plagiarism** — intellectual dishonesty — and a serious academic offense. *Plagiarism* comes from the Latin word *plagiarius*, which originally meant kidnapper and then was extended to cover literary or scholarly "kidnapping" of ideas or phrases as well.

Whenever you quote a source, you must put quotation marks around it — or, if it is long, omit quotation marks and indent it (see Section B) — and show where it came from:

As Jameson has said:

> For such an obsessed hero (whose prototype is of course Don Quixote), the apparent resistance of the real world can be easily accounted for by magic and the hostile operations of evil sorcerers: thus he never really comes in contact with outside reality, but only with the Utopian vision of it which was his starting point.[5]

Whenever you quote just a few words, perhaps paraphrasing the rest, you still must put quotation marks around the words you've quoted **and** show where the passage came from:

> Heroes like Don Quixote attribute the hostility of the world to "magic" or "operations of evil sorcerers"; these explanations make it possible for them to ignore the real world and confront only those worlds they have created.[5]

---

[5]The MLA now recommends referring to your sources in parentheses in the text, saving footnotes or endnotes for substantive discussions that do not fit into your text (like this one). These references would be keyed to an entry in your bibliography, giving the full title and publishing information; in this case to Fredric Jameson's Marxism and Form (Princeton: Princton UP, 1971). For further discussion of this method, see Section C.

Whenever you paraphrase or summarize a source, even if you do not quote any of the exact wording of the original, you must acknowledge that the ideas are not your own:

> Heroes like Don Quixote manage to ignore the claims of the real world by attributing its hostility to magic; they confront only the imaginary worlds they themselves have created.[5]

Your readers will expect footnotes or similar documentation for the following kinds of borrowing:

1. All word-for-word quotations (except common sayings)
2. All passages that you have summarized or paraphrased
3. All charts, graphs, diagrams that are not your own
4. All statistics that you have not compiled yourself
5. All theories or interpretations that are not your own
6. All key words or terms that you have taken from a specific source

B. When and how to quote

Students tend to use quotations more often than necessary. Often a paraphrase of your source, properly acknowledged, is adequate. Certainly you should never quote more than you are actually going to **use.** Don't quote a whole paragraph when all you are really interested in is a key phrase; don't reproduce a whole speech from *Hamlet* when you're only planning to discuss two or three lines. Quote only where the exact wording is crucial for your argument.

1. Quoting accurately. When you do need the exact words, you must give them exactly as they are written. Never change, add, or leave out something without showing what you've done. Your quotations must correspond exactly to the original, word for word, comma for comma, unless you indicate changes, omissions, or additions. The following quotation is from Lincoln's "Second Inaugural Address":

> With malice toward none, with charity for all, with
> firmness in the right as God gives us to see the
> right, let us strive on to finish the work we are in, to
> bind up the nation's wounds, to care for him who
> shall have borne the battle and for his widow and
> his orphan, to do all which may achieve and cherish
> a just and lasting peace among ourselves and with
> all nations.

Indicate omissions in your text by substituting an ellipsis (three spaced periods) for the words left out.

> As Lincoln said, "With malice toward none, with
> charity for all . . . let us strive on to finish the work
> we are in."

Be sure that your omissions do not distort or dest. ɔy the meaning, grammar, or syntax of the original. No ellipsis is necessary when your quotation is obviously a fragment:

> Lincoln's main concern at the end of the Civil War
> was "to bind up the nation's wounds."

Nor is an ellipsis necessary if your quotation can stand as a complete sentence.

   Indicate additions or changes by using square brackets (not parentheses, which could be understood to be part of the original text). These brackets are not in the repertoire of most typewriters and must be drawn in by hand.

> Lincoln hoped to help "him who shall have borne
> the battle [on either side] and . . . his widow and his
> orphan."

Often you will need to make minor changes, like the omission of *for* in the preceding example, to make the quotations fit your sentence. Sometimes, for example, you will have to change a pronoun and the tense of a verb:

> After Lincoln's death, the nation did "strive on to fin-
> ish the work [it was] in."

Indicate emphases not in the original text in parentheses after the quotation.

> In the speech, Lincoln constantly referred to the country as a whole: "Let us strive on to finish the work we are in, to bind up <u>the nation's</u> wounds" (emphasis added).

Otherwise your reader will assume that the writer had emphasized these words in the original, as Lincoln did elsewhere in the Second Inaugural Address.

Use *sic* — the Latin for *thus* or *so* — when you feel you must point out errors of fact, spelling, logic, or grammar in the original:

> Coleridge believed that literary works should have a "circular form, like the snake with it's [sic] tail in its mouth."

> One travel writer remarks that "in Jerusalem, where Christ was born [sic], East and West mingle."

*2. **Quoting prose.*** Incorporate prose quotations not more than four typed lines long in your text, as we have done with the brief quotations from Lincoln above. (If you use the quotation as part of your sentence, be sure it fits smoothly into your sentence structure. Don't insert a lengthy quotation in the middle of your sentence.) Longer prose quotations should be indented and single spaced, set off from the rest of your text by ten spaces at the left-hand margin, and separated from the body of your paper by a triple space at the beginning and end:

At the beginning of the Second Inaugural Address, Lincoln refers to his first address four years before:

> On the occasion corresponding to this four years ago all thoughts were anxiously directed to an impending war. All dreaded it, all sought to avert it. While the inaugural address was being delivered from this place, devoted altogether to <u>saving</u> the Union without war, insurgent agents were in the city seeking to

<u>destroy</u> it without war — seeking to dissolve the Union and divide effects by negotiation. Both parties deprecated war, but one of them would <u>make</u> war rather than let the nation survive, and the other would <u>accept</u> war rather than let it perish, and the war came.

Lincoln uses parallel structure throughout to underline the differences between the two parties.

You should use the same punctuation to introduce a quotation that you would use if it were all your own prose. If your introductory material flows directly into the quotation, no punctuation is necessary. If your introductory material is just a phrase *(As Lincoln said, Hegel writes,)* use a comma. If your introductory material is a complete sentence, use a colon to indicate that the following quotation is an example or clarification. Note, too, that quotation marks are not necessary around indented material.

3. Quoting poetry. Include brief quotations of poetry, a line or less, in quotation marks in your sentence.

The alliteration in "Then shall the fall further the flight in me" underlines the Christian paradox Herbert is exploring in "Easter Wings."

Two or three lines can also be included in your text. Separate the lines with a spaced slash and retain the capitalization of the original.

In "Easter Wings" Herbert hopes to "rise / As larks, harmoniously, / And sing this day thy victories."

If you need to quote more than three lines, however, you should center the poem on your page, indenting at least ten spaces, and separate the lines from your text by triple spacing on each side. Notice that you should reproduce not only the spelling, punctuation, and wording of the original but also the arrangement of the poem on the page as exactly as possible. Never run the lines into each other as if they were prose.

The shape of the first stanza of "Easter Wings" parallels

man's loss and subsequent hope:

> Lord, who created'st man in wealth and store,
>   Though foolishly he lost the same,
>   Decaying more and more
>   Till he became
>   Most poor;
>   With thee
>   Oh, let me rise
>   As larks, harmoniously,
>   And sing this day thy victories;
> Then shall the fall further the flight in me.

If your quotation begins in the middle of a line, you should leave it where it was on the page. Never move it to the left-hand margin of your quotation.

Herbert dramatizes man's dwindling "wealth and store":

>   he lost the same,
>   Decaying more and more
>   Till he became
>   Most poor.

The MLA Handbook for Writers of Research Papers, Theses, and Dissertations **(New York: Modern Language Association, 1984), Section 2.6, discusses more complex problems of quotation.**

C. Where and how to document

In short exercises and papers, when all your references are to a class text, you may simply indicate page numbers for quotations or references in parentheses. In short quotations, parentheses belong **after** the quotation mark and **before** final punctuation.

After Agathon's speech, Socrates says, sarcastically, "In my simplicity I imagined that the topic of praise should be true" (p. 324).

In long indented quotations, parentheses belong **after** the final punctuation.

For long poems numbered by line consecutively throughout, simply indicate the line numbers: ("Lycidas," 170-72). If a long poem is divided into books or cantos, use a capital Roman numeral for the book or canto, then give the line numbers: *(Paradise Lost,* III. 170-72). If a play is divided into acts and scenes, give the act with a capital Roman numeral, the scene with a small Roman numeral, and then the line numbers: *(Macbeth,* I. ii. 20-24). When you are writing about a novel, it is often simplest to give the number of the chapter your quotation is taken from. (You should **always** do this if you are not using a class text.)

When you refer to more than one source, however, this technique is inadequate. You must then deal with each reference separately, and include enough information so that your reader can find your sources in a library. There are many conventions for doing this. Sometimes you can include the entire bibliographic citation in the text; we used this method above. Sometimes you will use a raised numeral, a numeral in parentheses, or a short-form citation to refer your reader to the full information in a footnote, an endnote, or a bibliography. Your decision to use a particular format will depend on the conventions used by scholars in a particular academic discipline, on specific directions from your instructors, and sometimes on your own preference.

The conventions for referring to your sources, like all other human conventions, are arbitrary and often contradictory. In the style manuals of some of the academic disciplines taught at Smith College, for example, you can find the following contradictory pronouncements:

> *Capitalize only the first letter of the first word in the title of an article, chapter or book.* Capitalize all important words in the title.

> *Always give the complete title for an article in a journal.* Never give the title for an article in a journal.

Always give the full title of a journal. Always
abbreviate the journal title.

Give author's surname and initials. Give author's
full name.

But this does not mean that you are permitted to give your
references in a haphazard or inconsistent way. Quite the con-
trary. Like a peripatetic traveller, you must remember that,
although in China belching is a form of polite appreciation for a
meal, in America it is distinctly impolite. You must discover the
conventions that govern scholarly behavior in the academic field
in which you are writing, and then abide by them in detail
throughout your paper. We have included a commonly accepted
form for recording the sources you have used in a list of works
cited, or bibliography, and several different methods for reference to that list. (See the style manuals listed on pages 55-56 for
a fuller discussion of the methods preferred in each discipline.)
No matter what convention you follow, remember that your
goal should be to give your reader the necessary information as
clearly and as economically as possible. Never let your documentation become florid or fussy, an end in itself. Just give what your
reader needs to find or check your references quickly and easily.

D.   Listing the works you've used

At the end of your paper, you should include a list of the works
(books, articles, musical scores, computer software, unpub-
lished material — all your sources) you've used in writing your
paper. Arrange the entries alphabetically by author's last name
(or by title, if the work is anonymous). Give the author's last
name first, to make alphabetizing easier, and indent the following line or lines five spaces, to make the authors' last names
stand out. Double-space the entire list. The following schemes
and examples show both the kind of information you should
include and the correct order, spacing, and punctuation.

For a book:

Last Name, First Name. Full Title of Book: Subtitle. Series,

  if any. Place of Publication: Publisher, Year.

Jameson, Fredric. Marxism and Form: Twentieth Century

  Dialectical Theories of Literature. Princeton: Prin-

  ceton UP, 1971.

For an article in a periodical:

Last Name, First Name. "Title of Article: Subtitle." Name

  of Periodical Volume Number (Date): Pages.

Rorty, Amelie Oksenberg. "Experiments in Philosophic

  Genre: Descartes' Meditations." Critical Inquiry 9

  (1983): 545-64.

For an article in a book:

Last Name, First Name. "Title of Article." Title of Book. Ed.

  Editor's Name. Series, if any. Place of Publication:

  Publisher, Year. Pages.

Miller, Nancy K. "Writing (from) the Feminine: George

  Sand and the Novel of Female Pastoral." The

  Representation of Women in Fiction. Ed. Carolyn G.

  Heilbrun and Margaret R. Higonnet. Selected

  Papers from the English Institute, New Series 7.

  Baltimore: Johns Hopkins UP, 1983, 124-51.

When the book or article has more than one author, invert only the first name for alphabetizing. For further works by the same author, use three hyphens in place of the name; list alphabetically by title.

Jameson, Fredric. <u>Marxism and Form</u>. . . . (See above for

    full entry)

---. <u>The Prison-House of Language</u>: <u>A Critical Account of</u>

    <u>Structuralism and Russian Formalism</u>. Princeton:

    Princeton UP, 1977.

These are only examples of the most common entries. In general, use your common sense and these examples as a guide. For illustrations of rare forms — for citing everything from Congressional publications to record jackets — see the *MLA Handbook*, Sections 5.8.1-5.8.8.

E. Referring to your sources

Many, perhaps most, scholarly journals now recommend that you refer to your sources in parentheses within the text itself. (Footnotes and endnotes then are used only for substantive material that does not fit into your text or for a detailed discussion of your sources.) There are at least three systems for doing this: the author-page system, the author-date system, and the number system, all keyed to the list of works cited.

1. Author-page system: The most common system (recommended by the Modern Language Association, for example) gives just the author's name and the number of the page where you found the material.

Don Quixote "never really comes into contact with

outside reality, but only with that Utopian version of

it which was his starting point" (Jameson 174).

The information in parentheses (*after* quotation marks, *before* final punctuation) tells your reader that your quotation comes from page 174 of the work by Jameson listed in the Works Cited section at the end of your paper. All the publishing information the reader might need to locate your reference is there.

You should try to keep your parentheses as brief as possible. For example, if you include the author's name in your text, you need not include it in your parenthesis.

> Jameson believes that Don Quixote "never really comes into contact with outside reality" (174).

If you refer to the book as a whole, you only need to refer to the author's name. But if you include two or more works by the same author in your list of works cited, you will have to add a short title to identify the work you're referring to. For example, you might have used two of Jameson's books, both *Marxism and Form* and *The Prison-House of Language*. Then your reference should read:

> Don Quixote "never really comes into contact with outside reality" (Jameson, Marxism 174).

2. Author-date system:
Many journals in the social and physical sciences prefer that you refer to your sources by author and date, followed by a comma and the page where necessary: (Quigg 1985, 92). In the sciences the page number is often omitted, unless you are referring to a specific table or graph or are quoting directly.

If you follow this system, the Works Cited section must be changed slightly; the date of publication follows the author's name directly, for easy reference.

Quigg, Chris. 1985. "Elementary Particles and Forces." Scientific American 252: 84-95.

3. Number system: Some journals prefer references to a numbered bibliography. Following this system, you would simply give the *number* of the book or article you're referring to, often underlined, followed by the page: (14, 85).

The Works Cited section remains exactly the same as the entries given in Section 1, except that each entry is preceded by an Arabic numeral. In the sciences, the entries are often listed in the order in which they first appear in the text, instead of alphabetically.

14. Quigg, Chris. "Elementary Particles and Forces."

  Scientific American 252 (1985): 84-95.

4. Footnotes and endnotes: Until the early 1980s, most journals in the humanities recommended the use of footnotes or endnotes instead of parenthetical references. (You will still often find this method used, and your teacher may prefer it.) Under this system each time you refer to a book or article you must identify your reference with a raised Arabic numeral half a space above your line.

  Don Quixote "never comes into contact with outside

  reality, but only with that Utopian vision of it which

  was his starting point."[5]

Then give the source either at the bottom of the page — footnotes — or in a list at the end of your paper — endnotes. Number your notes consecutively throughout the paper.

The form of the reference differs only slightly from the form we've recommended above for the list of works cited. Do not invert the author's name (since you're not alphabetizing); do not separate the sections of the reference with periods; and put the publication information in parentheses.

For a book:

[1] First Name before Last Name, <u>Title of Book</u> (Place
of Publication: Publisher, Year) Page Number.

[5] Fredric Jameson, <u>Marxism and Form</u> (Princeton:
Princeton UP, 1971) 174.

For an article in a periodical:

[1] First Name before Last Name, "Title of Article,"
<u>Name of Periodical Volume</u> (Date): Page Number.

[3] Amelie Oksenberg Rorty, "Experiments in Philosophic Genre: Descartes' <u>Meditations</u>," <u>Critical
Inquiry</u> 9 (1983): 552-3.

For an article in a book-length collection:

[1] First Name before Last Name, "Title of Article," <u>Title
of Book,</u> ed. Name of Editor (Place of Publication:
Publisher, Year) Page Number.

[4] Nancy K. Miller, "Writing (from) the Feminine:
George Sand and the Novel of Female Pastoral," The
<u>Representation of Women in Fiction,</u> ed. Carolyn G.
Heilbrun and Margaret R. Higonnet (Baltimore:
Johns Hopkins UP, 1983) 126.

If you have already given a reference to a source in an earlier note, don't waste your time and your reader's by giving all the same information all over again. If you refer to only one book or article throughout your paper, give a full note the first time, then indicate the page number in your text, followed by a period.

> . . . "hostile operation of evil sorcerers" (174).

For later references when you are using more than one source, use the shortest possible note that will identify your source.

> [6]Jameson 22.

> [9]Miller 126.

For later references when you use more than one book or article by the same author, use the following form:

> [6]Jameson, Marxism 22.

> [10]Jameson, Prison-House 116.

Note that *Ibid.* (the same) and *op. cit.* (cited elsewhere) have disappeared from modern scholarly apparatus, though you will find them in older books and periodicals. If you use the note system, a list of works cited or bibliography is not really necessary in a short paper, though some teachers may require it.

F.   Other guides and style manuals:

Mary-Claire van Leunen's *Handbook for Scholars* (New York: Knopf, 1979) is the best example we know of thorough, intelligent, and irreverent thinking about scholarly conventions.

When you decide on your major, you should buy the style manual that is accepted in your discipline. Most journals in the humanities and some social sciences follow the forms recommended in one of the two following style manuals:

Modern Language Association. *MLA Handbook for Writers of Research Papers*. 2nd ed., revised. New York: Modern Language Association, 1984.

Chicago Manual of Style. 13th ed. Chicago: U of Chicago P, 1982.

Manuals for specific fields include the following:

Biology

Council of Biology Editors. Style Manual Committee. *CBE Style Manual: A Guide for Authors, Editors, and Publishers in the Biological Sciences*. 5th ed. Bethesda: Council of Biology Editors, 1983.

Chemistry

American Chemical Society. *Handbook for Authors of Papers in American Chemical Society Publications*. Washington: American Chemical Society, 1978.

Association of Official Analytic Chemists. *The AOAC Style Manual*. Washington: 1972.

Geology

American Geological Institute. *Geowriting: A Guide to Writing, Editing, and Printing in Earth Science*. Washington: 1973.

United States Geological Survey. *Suggestions to Authors of the Reports of the United States Geological Survey*. 6th ed. Washington: GPO, 1978.

Mathematics

American Mathematical Society. *A Manual for Authors of Mathematical Papers*. 7th ed. Providence: American Mathematical Society, 1980.

Physics

American Institute of Physics. Publications Board. *Style Manual for Guidance in the Preparation of Papers*. 3rd ed. New York: American Institute of Physics, 1978.

Psychology

American Psychological Association. *Publication Manual of the American Psychological Association*. 3rd ed. Washington: American Psychological Association, 1983.

V. Editing Yourself

Remember that re-vision suggests seeing again, looking at your paper in a new way. Learn to criticize your own work before you hand it in; after all, you won't always have people around who are paid to correct your prose.

Before final typing

1. Write a one-paragraph summary of your paper. If your paper is vague or rambling or pointless, your summary will reveal its flaws.

2. Read your paper aloud — to anyone you can find who will listen. Is it easy or awkward to read? How does it sound? (If you find clumsy or monotonous parts, rewrite them.) Ask your listener to summarize your paper. Are you pleased with the summary, or does it miss your point? If the summary seems unsatisfactory, change your organization, your emphasis, your last paragraph to make your points clear.

3. Circle all forms of the verb *to be* in your draft: *is, are, was, were*, etc. Then go back to see how many you can eliminate. (Weak passives and weak constructions like *there are* should disappear.) Check tenses, too.

4. Underline your transitional words, phrases, and sentences, particularly between paragraphs. Do you lead your readers from point to point, or do you expect your readers to make their own connections? If transitions are missing, add sentences or connecting phrases to show the relationship between your points. If your transitions seem ponderous or mechanical, simplify or omit them.

5. Check your word choice in the first paragraph. Do you use many long, Latinate words or filler phrases? Could you say things more directly? If so, revise your paragraph — and check the rest of your paper too. (This is a good time to check spelling as well.)

6. Consider your first and last paragraphs. If your readers had only these, would they be able to tell what the subject of your paper is? and how you have developed that subject? If not, rewrite them. Do you just mark time in your first paragraph? Does your last paragraph simply repeat what you have said in the first one? If so, rewrite them.

7. Check all quotations to make sure they are exact. Have you given credit where it is due? Are your notes and bibliography accurate?

8. Check comments on recent papers. Have you made any of the same old mistakes?

Typing

9. Use standard typing paper — not very thin or easily smeared. (If you find it convenient to type on erasable paper, hand in a photocopy on plain paper.) Double-space, and leave margins of about an inch and one-half at top, bottom, and sides. Number pages consecutively in the upper right-hand corner. (Imagine what would happen if someone dropped your paper.) Fasten your pages with a sturdy paper clip or staple — not a safety pin, plastic cover, or bulky binder (unless your paper is very bulky). Be sure to follow any specific directions your teacher has given.

After typing

10. Proofread your paper carefully, comparing it with your original. (This proofreading is usually very hard to do, but do it anyway.) Get a friend to help. Have you omitted any words, sentences, even paragraphs? Correct mistakes by crossing out the whole word and writing the correct form above it **in ink.** Remember you — not your typewriter or your typist — are responsible for the final state of your paper.

Index